Maren Muter

Maren Muter

The Story of Cacao

Printed in the United States of America
Edited, formatted, and interior design by Maren Muter Cover art Inspired by Claudia Farnety
Muter, Maren The Story of Cacao / Maren
p. cm.

ISBN: 978-1-7321128-4-1
First edition published 2026 10 9 8 7 6 5 4 3 2 1 0

Once upon a time in a rainforest hidden from the outside world,
a curious tree grew beneath the lush canopy.

It was adorned with delicate flowers and painted vibrantly with mysterious pods.

The tiny flowers were lovely,
like angels floating on the bark of the tree.

They grew by the thousands and held their breath, were shy.
They had no perfume, no flashy colors.

Nothing to intrigue a suitor.

The bees flew right passed.
The butterflies didn't look twice.

Only the wind noticed.

It directed tiny midge flies into the flowers. And, carrying pollen with them, they jumped back into the wind.

Periodically, one of the midge flies was
blown into another flower.

With this process, it was amazing that even three flowers were
pollinated for every thousand.

But they were, and they grew.

Soon, the tree was bursting with beautiful green,
yellow, orange, red, and purple pods.

The pods resembled the skin of an old woman, as though a thousand ancient stories rippled deeply across their surfaces.

Inside the pods, purple and ivory beans were wrapped in a thick pulp that tasted like a fragrant lemon sorbet.

In the forest, animals were drawn to the curious tree.

They plucked the pods to taste the tales.

And, sucked on the pulp throwing the beans aside.

But the beans didn't mind. The earth felt good.

Blankets of leaves wrapped them.
They listened to the melody of life, and sprouted.

The legend of people's first encounter with cacao took place just a few degrees north of the equator in 9000 BC when the indigenous people happened upon the little grove of curious trees.

They watched the animals savor the tastes and joined in.

It opened their palate with gentle flavors of fruit, sweet and tangy, with whispered depths of umami.

It filled their hearts.

Below the trees, music abound as the untouched pods were hardened like wood with their beans rattling within.

This is what happened to the pods when they went untouched.

The pulp inside heated up and melted through a fermentation process; acids broke through the cellular walls of the beans, killing them.

Rendering them useless.

Then the hull absorbed the liquid pulp and petrified itself before falling to the ground.

It seems life can feel this way too.

40

Sometimes, it seems as if life is hard or unfair.
Sometimes, others can feel worthless, unwanted, or hurt.

And, their shells harden.

They often try to put on a smile and pretend all is well while inside their hearts are rattling.

One day, all those thousands of years ago, as the people were in ceremony, one of the petrified pods broke open.

...and the useless beans fell out.

A alchemist stepped forward and gathered them.

He placed them in a mortar and pestle,
and ground them into paste.

With a touch of honeyed water, he brought the paste to his lips.

And the world opened before him.

The gods had sent a message through the life of those curious
trees and opened the minds and souls of those who drank.

From what looked and seemed as something
practically worthless, the inside of that petrified pod ended up
holding one of the most coveted substances of all time.

With a value far greater than gold.

The gift of chocolate is the gift of life.

And offers a great secret.

Without all of those tiny flowers, without the encouragement
of the wind for the rare brush of the midge fly...

Without the touch and desire of the animals, or the wrapping of the forest floor, the pods don't open, and the beans don't grow.

And, only through the fermentation process and breaking down the cellular walls, is the power of cocoa is released.

But, it offers even more magic. Through it you will find that even though someone or something is rendered useless.

Look again.

Beneath what may look wrinkled, or undesired, or broken.

There is a spirit that resides...

Holding the most special thing of all.

You.

Maren Muter

Somewhere along the path less traveled, my heart it led, four directions baffled. Should we meet before the end, this gift of chocolate for you, my friend.

—Maren